Robert's Rules

The Ultimate Guide to Understanding and Practicing Robert's Rules of Order

Elliot J. Smith

© Copyright 2016 by Elliot J. Smith - All rights reserved.

This document is geared towards providing exact and reliable information in regards to the topic and issue covered. The publication is sold with the idea that the publisher is not required to render accounting, officially permitted, or otherwise, qualified services. If advice is necessary, legal or professional, a practiced individual in the profession should be ordered.

- From a Declaration of Principles which was accepted and approved equally by a Committee of the American Bar Association and a Committee of Publishers and Associations.

In no way is it legal to reproduce, duplicate, or transmit any part of this document in either electronic means or in printed format. Recording of this publication is strictly prohibited and any storage of this document is not allowed unless with written permission from the publisher. All rights reserved.

The information provided herein is stated to be truthful and consistent, in that any liability, in terms of inattention or otherwise, by any usage or abuse of any policies, processes, or directions contained within is the solitary and utter responsibility of the recipient reader. Under no circumstances will any legal responsibility or blame be held against the publisher for any reparation, damages, or monetary loss due to the information herein, either directly or indirectly.

Respective authors own all copyrights not held by the publisher.

The information herein is offered for informational purposes solely, and is universal as so. The presentation of the information is without contract or any type of guarantee assurance.

The trademarks that are used are without any consent, and the publication of the trademark is without permission or backing by the trademark owner. All trademarks and brands within this book are for clarifying purposes only and are the owned by the owners themselves, not affiliated with this document.

Contents

INTRODUCTION 1

CHAPTER 1 FOUNDATION FOR SUCCESS 3

CHAPTER 2 CREATING THE BYLAWS 19

CHAPTER 3 A PROPER MEETING 32

CHAPTER 4 MOTIONS EXPLAINED 44

CHAPTER 5 CREATING SUCCESSFUL COMMITTEES .. 51

CHAPTER 6 ROLES AND RESPONSIBILITIES 64

Introduction

Chances are, you have been to a meeting where you felt like your voice wasn't heard, or you weren't even given the opportunity to be heard. The most likely culprit for this occurrence is disorganization, which leads to confusion. There were probably many different people trying to talk over one another, especially if the topic of the meeting was controversial. Even the most innocent of meetings can get rather argumentative if not monitored properly.

This is why Robert's Rules of Order is so important; it sets the groundwork for a properly held meeting regardless of size or harmony. These rules are based on parliamentary law but are not to be confused with a law book, because they are not. Instead, Robert's Rules of Order is meant for ordinary people, not legislative assemblies; this is what sets it apart from other rule books. It is meant to adapt to any situation we face when it comes to organized meetings, from church to work.

If Robert's Rules of Order is followed, everyone, including the minority, is given a chance to speak. When everyone has a voice and is given the chance to have the floor, meetings will run more smoothly. It is important that everyone has a copy of the rules and understands how to follow them. This will make the meeting more efficient and help avoid confusion. In the beginning, it might seem difficult to follow the rules, but with some determination and dedication, your meetings will start to flow naturally without anyone being left out.

Chapter 1
Foundation for Success

When you are starting an organization, you might feel overwhelmed with how to hold your board meetings and the steps you must take. You probably have an idea of how you want your meeting to go – as smoothly as possible. However, you just aren't sure where to start to make it happen. This is why Robert's Rules of Order will help; this book will show you how to use these rules to make your meetings operate as smoothly as possible, from start to finish.

If you are starting a new organization, be prepared to dedicate a lot of time and effort to the cause. When starting out, continuity and procedure are very important to achieving your vision. It is important to keep track of your ideas and to be patient, Rome was not built in a day, and the same goes for a well-made organization. If you are embarking on this mission alone, you are probably going to feel overwhelmed numerous times throughout the creation process. This is normal and expected; you are building a club or organization from the ground up, after all. However, the more educated you are, the more likely you are to be successful.

Guidelines for starting a new organization:

Decisions. When you are planning your first meeting, you will have a lot of decisions to make. If you are doing this in a group, make sure everyone is heard. It is important that everyone agrees, as this will increase your chances of success. Some of the things that must be discussed during this planning phase are: when and where the meetings will be held, how you are going to publicize the meetings, and the specifics of Robert's Rules so that everyone in the group understands exactly how the meeting will proceed.

You will also need to think about prospective members. If you already have a list of those who want to be members, this task does not apply to you. If you don't have a list, come up with a way to let others know about the organization and how they can join. Some common ways to do this are through social media, fliers, or even taking an ad out in the paper. You will also need to come up with your own set of bylaws, which we will discuss in detail later.

The importance of the bylaws cannot be stressed enough, as they will act as a guide and contain the answers to nearly any question a person has. That means there is a lot to include. If the bylaws are not thorough, any number of issues can arise with respect to the flow of the organization, from the duties of the officers to whether bills are paid using cash or check. As you read this book, pay attention to all the times when bylaws are mentioned; this will help you when you start building yours.

Meetings

To organize a meeting, you need a meeting to organize. That seems like common sense, but it's easy for someone to be overlooked or to not give enough notice. That is one of the reasons why these rules exist – to prevent things like this from happening. Since these rules are made for any type of group, they are meant to be both universal and customizable.

According to the rules, each voting member has the right to have prior notice of a meeting. The basis of the rules is that everyone has a voice, and for that to happen, everyone must be given notice about the meetings. Think of it like this: you can't attend a meeting if you don't know about it. Depending on what your group is meeting about and who is involved, legal requirements might exist with respect to lengths of notice (examples of this are town council or school board meetings). If this is the case, it is up to you to know the appropriate schedule so that you can give enough notice. In addition, if your meeting is informal, you can choose what you feel is a proper schedule.

Regardless of the purpose of the meeting, your notice about it must contain some basic elements:

Time

Location

Specifications of all items of business, such as proposals to amend existing bylaws or to rescind or amend something adopted previously.

The type of notice you give will depend on what type of meeting it is:

Regular Meetings: This type of meeting has a routine schedule and is open for typical business matters that must be discussed. The delivery and content requirements for regular meetings are generally explained in the bylaws. This is true for most public meetings, but if not, when you are making the schedule, take the frequency of the meetings, the importance of the meeting, and the distance all members will need to travel into consideration when setting the lead time. Your goal with the notice is to give all members enough time to receive the notice, change their schedules if necessary, and make travel arrangements so they can attend, since it is their right as voting members to do so.

Special Meetings: These are not regularly scheduled meetings; they are more like emergency meetings. Special meetings are generally held if something that is both time-sensitive and important comes up that cannot wait until the regularly scheduled meeting. Previous notice MUST be given for these types of meetings, and they too must contain the date, time, and location of the meeting. Special meeting notices must contain a description of the business that will be discussed during the meeting – basically, the reason why the special meeting is being held in the first place. Special meetings can include only those topics of business mentioned in the notice – nothing else.

Tip: As a precaution, double check your bylaws to make sure you are mailing notices within the specified time frame before the scheduled meeting. For instance, "Notice of special meetings must be sent to all members at least two weeks, but no more than four weeks, before the meeting."

Of course, the length of time for the notice will vary because of the size of the group and the distance members must travel; both should be taken into consideration when bylaws are written.

There are different ways to give notice; these will depend on the rules of the organization:

Announcement: This is a simple oral notice, given at a regular meeting, about the next meeting time. This works best for small, informal groups that have frequent meetings.

Fixed Rule: Some bylaws have a set time and place for a meeting that changes only for special meetings. An example of this is a "regular meetings of the Black and White Movie Club will be held on the second Wednesday of every month at 7 p.m. at Bob's Diner." These meetings are already set, so the notice itself is built into the bylaws, which would be discussed when a person joins the group.

Mailing: This method of giving notice can include a text message, an email, or traditional mail. Regardless of the method of distribution, the notice must reach each person at the specified time and include all the necessary information.

Everyone must agree to the method of distribution.

Remember: Traditionally, unless agreed upon, electronic notification is not considered a good faith effort to contact members. Check your bylaws to see if they contain information regarding the acceptable methods of distribution. Not everyone has access to electronic communications. Although this is changing, some groups still require more traditional means of distribution in addition to the electronic notice.

Officers:

Robert's Rules gives you different options when it comes to electing temporary officers who will preside over the meeting. The voting process can be carried out by ballot, voice, or roll call. The most-used option is ballot because it can be less confusing than voice, which can quickly become chaotic, especially if the group is large.

The first step is nominating candidates for the various positions. For your first meeting, you might already have a chair chosen because it will be the first time that members of your group have met with one another. However, if this is not the case, there are different ways to make nominations:

By the Chair: This method works when members want to rely on the presiding officer to suggest candidates, but the members also want to approve of the nominee.

Floor: This is often referred to as "open nominations" and is the best-known method. This method is most commonly used when the process of electing officers at a meeting is left up to the members. Some bylaws prevent this type of nomination from occurring, so make sure this is acceptable. Nominations can be made by any member. This can take place when an election is still pending or during a meeting before the election meeting. Choosing when you want to hold the nominations should depend on what fits best with your group's schedule.

Floor nominations must follow these rules:

It is not necessary for the chair to recognize a nominee, but if you are doing this by voice, it can be tricky and confusing. If you have a big group, choosing a different, more formal process might be more appropriate (for instance, having members write down their nominees).

It is not a requirement that nominations be seconded, but it is certainly not uncommon for this to happen. This is just an agreement and the signal most people will use to show their endorsement.

Members should not make more than one nomination to a position when there are multiple seats for the same office. For example, with nominees to a board, each member should have an opportunity to give his or her nomination for the one specific position before moving on to the nominations for the next positions.

If it is not prohibited in the bylaws, a person can be nominated for more than one office and if elected for both can even serve on both.

Nominations go in the order specified in the bylaws.

Open nominations usually do not require a specific close; they end when no one else has a nomination to make. When this happens, it is up to the chair to declare the nominations closed, a task usually done asking the members three times.

Committee: Some groups use a nominating committee to put together a list of qualified and willing candidates. This can be very beneficial to members when it comes to selecting officers, especially in large groups, because it can save a lot of time. Generally, the bylaws state that the committee only choose people who have expressed interest in a position, who are willing to do the job, and who are qualified for any offices for which they are nominated.

Ballot: This is another method that incorporates the principle of allowing all voters to make nominations, but this time it is done by ballot. The ballots are then tallied, similar to an election ballot. Once the list has been created, it will be the list of nominees for each office. This method gives members an idea of the preferences of the group without holding an actual election.

Mail: This is very similar to the ballot method, but this technique requires that extra measures be taken to protect the privacy of the ballot. This is usually specified in the bylaws, so make sure to check before you give the members instructions. If this is not the case, one of the best ways to ensure privacy is to have each member put his or her folded ballot in a signed envelope, then put this envelope in an outer envelope which will then be mailed. The inner envelopes will be checked against a list of the names of voters to make sure everyone is accounted for. It is then tallied and a list is made, just as with the ballot method.

Petition: Some organizations will allow only nominations that have been submitted on a petition with a certain number of members. Nominating people by petition can also be done by mail or in person. This is customarily stated in the bylaws. Everyone must have access to the petitions and the forms to start a petition. This is important because every voting member has the right to sign.

Election:

Once the list of nominees has been made, it is time to elect officers. This is done in a manner very similar to selecting the nominees. Robert's Rules makes an election a simple process, treating it as nothing more than the following through of a motion. In the case of an election, it is answering the question of who will fill a certain position.

Ballot: This is the best method to allow for free expression of the members.

This method can be approached in two ways: nominations are finished before balloting starts, which can save time and be done at a time and place that is not a meeting. However, the disadvantage of this approach is that a candidate can lose an election for a position that was decided earlier and then they can't serve in a different position. To avoid this problem, make it clear to the members that a person who is nominated for two positions can also be elected to and serve in two positions. They can then choose to accept the positions to which they have been elected or choose only one.

The other approach is to have the election for a particular office right after the nomination. The main benefit of this is that it lets members consider the results before they move on to the election of a different office. When groups use this method, the nominations are taken and then followed by the election. The drawback of this is that it is more time consuming. For this reason, it is best for smaller groups.

Regardless of which procedure you choose, the order of the elections should be outlined in the bylaws. Voting by ballot also allows members to vote for someone who has not been formally nominated as long as the person is real and the name can be read. This is known as a write-in vote.

Voice: This method is not as commonly used, but if the group is not opposed and the bylaws allow it, the voice method can be less time consuming than the ballot method. Once the nominations are closed, votes are taken and counted on each nominee in the order of the nominations. This approach can show favoritism to one candidate over another because of the order of the nominations, so it should be used only in large meetings or if there is not a very serious contest for an office.

Roll Call: This method is used if members are held accountable to a constituency. The procedure is the same as ballot voting right up until the time comes to fill out the ballot. Instead, the secretary will call each person's name; the person will then give his or her vote. The secretary will repeat the vote before logging it.

Who Wins?

The majority vote determines the winner unless the bylaws specify differently. In a voice vote, the winner is easily determined and the voting is automatically over if someone has the majority vote. Ballot elections are not finished until a position is filled, and this can happen only when a candidate receives the majority. If there are only two candidates and a tie occurs, the process is repeated until one candidate receives a majority.

When it comes to ballot voting, it is not acceptable to drop the candidates who have received the lowest votes unless they voluntarily withdraw. This means run-offs are not allowed. A candidate on a ballot who is receiving low votes is not obligated to withdraw because members could still vote for this particular person as a compromise candidate.

Permanent Resolution

A resolution or rule can be adopted as permanent by a quick vote during any regular session or meeting. Of course, for it to be adopted, it must win the majority and it will continue until it is rescinded. If you would like a rule to be more permanent, it can also be voted on to be added to the bylaws, which requires more than a simple majority vote to be rescinded. To vote something into the bylaws, a two-thirds vote is usually necessary.

Adjourning a Meeting

The words "I declare the meeting adjourned" by the chair signify that the meeting has been closed. However, two situations exist when closing can take place without a motion:

- The time set for adjournment has been reached. The chair will then announce the time and unless someone quickly moves to set aside the orders of the day, the meeting can be closed with a simple declaration.

- Everything on the agenda has been completed. The chair will ask if anyone has anything else to discuss. If no one speaks up, the chair can declare the meeting adjourned.

It doesn't matter how loud the "ayes" are; a meeting cannot be adjourned until the chair declares it. The motion to adjourn is simple and comes in three forms:

- Now: "Mr. President, I move to adjourn." A quick vote is taken and acceptance of the motion will immediately close the meeting.

- Later: "Mr. President, I move to adjourn to meet again tomorrow at 9 a.m." A vote will be taken again and, if accepted, the meeting will continue at the agreed-upon time.

- Sine die/Without day: "Mr. Chairman, I move to adjourn sine die." This is used to finish the final meeting of a convention of delegates.

In the time between when the motion is adopted and when the chair makes the declaration, the following are still permitted: making important announcements, providing notice for future motions, setting the time for an adjourned meeting, and sharing information about something that requires attention before adjournment.

As you can see, Robert's Rules provides you with many different options so you can tailor nearly every aspect of running the organization to your specific needs. This gives you more freedom to create the kind of club you have always wanted.

Chapter 2
Creating the Bylaws

Now it is time to create your own set of bylaws. This can seem like a daunting task, especially in the beginning, but there are ways to make it easier on yourself. This chapter will help you build a set of comprehensive bylaws that work for your organization. The best bylaws are detailed and incredibly thorough. They will contain information about every aspect of the organization. As a matter of fact, as you read this book, you will see just how often bylaws are referenced; it will probably surprise you.

First, you need to know what bylaws are and why they are so important. According to Robert's Rules, bylaws are used to define an organization and explain members' rights. There is a basic list, but your finalized set of bylaws should contain more than the basics because this is how the bylaws are tailored to your organization. Bylaws are important because they answer any questions about procedures. This is especially important for new members who are just learning about how the organization operates; a proper set of bylaws will give them all the necessary information.

This is the basic list:

Name: This is the official name of the organization.

Object: This article will include the purpose of the group. It should be broad enough to address the things you do as a group. However, numbering details should be avoided because if you list things, should something be forgotten, it will be considered excluded.

Membership: This article should include information about the different types of memberships and classes and the voting rights of these various groups. This section should also include eligibility requirements, including special procedures for admission. In addition, this section will include details about fees or dues, the due dates of these fees, restrictions of delinquent members, explanations of when members are released from the group for nonpayment and any reinstatement rights. This article will also include information regarding resignations or any complex necessities in relation to memberships in superior organizations.

Officers: This article is where you will need to explain the specifications of the officers in the organization, such as a detailed description of their duties. You will need to include qualifications of the candidates and details about the nomination process, the election, and the terms of office. In this section, you can also indicate whether a limit on consecutive terms exists. Rules for filling vacancies and succession must be included here as well. A separate article should be made detailing the duties of each officer.

Meetings: This article will include the schedule for the regular meetings. Rules regarding special meetings such as lead times will also need to be included here. You must consider by whom and how special meetings can be called. The minimum number of members required to hold a meeting should be included in this article as well.

Executive Board: Even though this is part of the basic list, not every organization chooses to have an executive board. If you choose not to, skip this article. However, if this applies to you, include the details about your board here. It is important that you be clear and specific about who is on the board, when they meet, and all the special rules that apply to the board. The board must have limits to its powers, and these limitations should be explained in detail here.

Committees: This article should contain a definition of all the committees your group anticipates it will need to carry out business in separate sections. You should include the names of the committees, how the members will be selected, and the role each committee has within the organization. Think about the future; it is smart to include information about how to add committees, such as who will authorize the formation of a new standing committee. If you do not include this information but decide to add a committee later, the bylaws must be amended. With that in mind, it is easier to simply include this procedure in the initial bylaws.

Parliamentary Authority: This is the place where you will specify what parliamentary authority you have chosen to incorporate. An example of this is Robert's Rules. You must include this information so members can do their own research if they have questions.

Amendment: In this article goes information about how the group will amend the bylaws. You will need to include the specific requirements and what constitutes the majority necessary to change the bylaws. If you do not have any special procedures, Robert's Rules requires a two-thirds vote and previous notice.

As you can see, this is a very basic set of bylaws; it still leaves out a lot of important information. To customize the bylaws for your organization, you will need to add more bylaws that relate to your group and its purpose.

Remember, if the bylaws don't authorize it, you simply can't do it.

You might not know where to start; this is a checklist that will help you add what is necessary to make your bylaws more comprehensive and fitting for your organization. However, this is just a basic list; what you include in your bylaws will depend on your specific needs and wants. This is a great jumping-off point, but when you are creating your bylaws, avoid vague statements. Doing this will ensure that members and officers know exactly what is expected of them and how to follow procedures to your specifications. There is a reason bylaws differ so drastically; everyone has his or her vision and ideas about how an organization should operate, and uses the bylaws to make this happen. What works in one club might not work in another, even if the purpose is similar.

Type of elections: cumulative, preferential, or plurality.

How to submit absentee votes, the procedure.

How to hold a runoff between the top two candidates.

The process of suspending a requirement for a ballot vote.

How to suspend a bylaw.

Whether you want to limit officers to those who are members.

Restrictions on write-in votes.

How to prevent a vice president from taking the office of president if there is a vacancy.

Whether honorary members or officers are allowed to vote.

What the dues will go towards and how much the dues will be.

How to suspend or drop a member due to nonpayment.

Whether meetings can be held electronically.

Procedures for holding special meetings.

When you go through this checklist, think about who the potential members will be and what the organization is. For instance, a historical group might have higher dues than a movie club. The time of notice might need to be longer if your members live far from the meeting place. This is how you can customize the bylaws to fit your needs. If you are starting your organization with a group, make sure to listen to everyone's suggestions. It is better to have more details in your bylaws than too few.

Bylaws vs. Rules of Order

Even though both basically serve the same functional purpose, they work together and are not interchangeable. Bylaws are written and agreed upon by those who created the organization. They explain how business will be conducted and how decisions will be made within the group. The use of bylaws suggests a commitment to following a parliamentary procedure such as Robert's Rules. Rules of order or standing rules are more administrative in nature, including information about conduct such as the use of petty cash.

The biggest difference between the two relates to scope. Bylaws are not meant to be easy to alter, while rules of order can be changed during a regular meeting through a simple majority vote. The best way to think about it is this: rules are specific and administrative; if they do not seem to be working, they can be changed easily. An example of this is changing the location of meetings because of nearby construction. Bylaws are meant to be procedural and encompassing; amendments to them are supposed to be time consuming and complex. Otherwise, there would be no use for bylaws at all and rules of order would be used for all operations.

Amending the Bylaws

It is inevitable that you will need to amend your bylaws at some point. Change is a part of life and your organization is no exception. When you need to amend a bylaw, just accept it and remember that you have already planned for this. Even though bylaws are not meant to be easily amended, a procedure exists that will make it happen.

Every member should have the opportunity to provide his or her opinion about the change. Robert's Rules gives everyone a voice, after all. A bylaw cannot be changed if a minority larger than one-third does not agree with the proposal. Robert's Rules requires previous notice and at least a two-thirds vote to amend a bylaw. In addition, if you have any other requirements you added to your specific bylaws, these, too, must be met.

When you amend your bylaws, you are basically changing the contract between members and how the organization operates. Making these changes requires you to be technical and precise, so pay close attention to the procedure laid out in the bylaws. When an amendment is proposed, three components must be included:

- A precisely worded proposed amendment.

- The existing bylaw.

- How the new bylaw will read if adopted.

The name(s) of the proposing member or members should be included, as should the reason why they are suggesting the amendment.

Approaching members with the amendment is considered a special application to the motion and is subject to existing rules. This means that two people cannot speak at the same time and that everyone can share his or her ideas about the amendment. However, once you have adopted the amendment, the vote cannot be reconsidered. This would require that the process be started all over again because it would be considered its own separate amendment. That is why the voting requirements must be met, whether those requirements are what was set in your bylaws or are two-thirds of the vote.

It is not necessary to amend an entire article of your bylaws, but it would still be approached as a main motion. Examples of this would be:

- Striking out sentences, paragraphs, or words.

- Inserting sentences, paragraphs, or words.

- Substituting sentences, paragraphs, or words.

If need be, a full rewrite of the bylaws is an option; this can drastically change the structure of the organization. If you or someone is proposing this, for everything that is being changed, a substitution should be included. Basically, this means that someone cannot want to change the bylaws without providing an alternative. All members should receive a hard copy of the revisions, and everyone is allowed to share their thoughts and ideas about the revision.

The results of the vote will be recorded in the minutes.

Asking a Professional

If you are faced with creating the bylaws yourself or if you feel like your bylaws are not thorough enough, you can go to a professional for help. You do not have to do this, but for beginners, this can be a very helpful tool. The best place to find a professional is the National Association of

Parliamentarians. They provide services and products to help the general public participate in or manage meetings. They also offer accreditation and continuing education. You do not have to do this, but know that if you feel overwhelmed and in need of help, it is there.

Some people opt out of hiring a professional and choose to instead join a group that also incorporates Robert's Rules. This allows them to experience what it is like to be a new member, as well as to see the rules in action. This will give you personal experience with how a club operates; it will also give you ideas for your own club. Not liking certain aspects is just as helpful because you will know what to avoid. Again, there are so many different options and combinations to consider that you might feel overwhelmed until you gain hands-on experience.

Just like when you were in school, you are learning a new subject. Try not to be too hard on yourself during the learning process. Instead, focus on doing the best you can. If you are eager and enthusiastic about learning, it will show and you will increase your chances of success. Keep this in mind throughout the whole process. A positive attitude will also motivate you when things get rough and you feel like quitting, which will probably happen. However, you know organizations and clubs exist, so realistically there is no reason you can't be one of the people who starts one.

Chapter 3
A Proper Meeting

Now it is time to hold your meetings, but what exactly should be covered? Of course, every organization serves a different purpose, so no two meetings will be the same. However, a general set of guidelines exists to help your meetings run smoothly. One of the easiest ways to remember this is to follow the 3R-SUN format:

Reading of minutes.

Reports of standing committees, boards, and officers.

Reports of special committees.

Special orders or announcements.

Unfinished orders or business.

New business or announcements.

That is the most simplified explanation of a successful meeting. However, it is much easier if you have attended a full meeting so you can see it in action. The following is an example of a meeting from start to finish so you can see in greater detail how Robert's Rules works based on a president's scripted agenda.

Date: February 16, 2016

Call to Order

2:00 p.m.

Gavel rap one time.

"The meeting will come to order."

Correction or Approval of Minutes

Officer or Chairman: "A draft of the secretary's minutes from the January meeting was sent to everyone last week. A copy is also in your meeting packet. Did anyone find any errors in the script?"

Pause.

"Does anyone have any corrections to add to the minutes that were distributed?"

Take all corrections until none are left.

"If there no more corrections, the minutes are now approved as distributed."

"The officer reports are our next order of business."

Reports of Officers

"Everyone has a copy of my written report. I will go over a couple of the important points and we can move on."

Treasurer's Report

"The Chair recognizes (name) as treasurer for report."

"Thank you, (name)."

"We have 97 dues-paid members, $12,346 total cash accounts. The financial reports for the next period (dates) are in your meeting packets. Also in your packet is an income and expense report that covers the year to date if anyone has any questions."

Answer Questions

"No action is necessary regarding the treasurer's report, so it will be filed for audit."

"Before we continue, I am going to report some committee appointments."

Any appointments will be described.

Executive Director's Report

"The Chair recognizes (name) for the report."

"Thank you, (name)."

"There are many recommendations and we will look at them one at a time . . ."

The secretary will be asked to read the first recommendation. Someone will then "move the adoption of the recommendation just read."

State the motion

"It is moved to adopt the recommendation that was just read. Do we need to debate?"

The chairman will handle the discussion if there is a debate. When ready:

"Those in favor, say 'Aye.'"

Pause.

"Those opposed, say 'No.'"

Pause.

The responses are counted and, based on the number, the following will be stated.

"The motion fails (or passes) and the recommendation is not (or is) adopted."

"Our next order of business is the standing committee reports."

Standing Committee Reports

The name of a specific committee is included here; this, of course, depends on the organization.

"The Chair recognizes (name) for the committee report."

The script for motions based on the specific committee is given.

"Thank you, (name)."

This will continue until all standing and special committees have given their reports.

New Business

"Is there new business?"

"The chair recognizes (name)."

This person makes a motion and it is seconded.

"It is moved and seconded to create a new special committee consisting of four members to be appointed by the president to report recommendations on the needs of the continuing education of existing members." (This is just an example.)

If there is a debate, it is handled and put to question; the result is announced.

"Is there any other business that needs to be handled?"

Pause.

Other business is handled in the same way.

Announcements

"It has come to my attention that we must set the date for the next meeting. March 16th is the normal date. Should we keep the set date? Hearing no objections, we shall meet on March 16th at 2 p.m. here at the restaurant."

If there are other announcements, they will be made during this time.

Adjourn

"If there is no further business, the meeting is adjourned."

This is how smoothly your meetings should go when using Robert's Rules. Everyone is given a chance to speak when debates are introduced, and the next order of business begins once all debates or questions have been answered. As discussed in the previous chapter, some meetings will run over, and it is necessary to motion or a later date.

This can happen for many reasons, such as an abundance of questions or a long list of announcements that causes the meeting to run too long. Many people think this is negative, but that is not always the case. Sometimes there is just too much to cover in the set amount of time.

The business matters and recommendations discussed during a meeting will vary depending on the type of organization. For instance, a church might be having a bake sale or rally day, and that is the topic of their business for that meeting, while a movie club might be hosting a kid's movie night and choosing an age-appropriate film might be the topic of their business. The type of organization or club you have will determine what is discussed during the meetings. The previous was simply an example of how a regular meeting will flow from start to finish so you have an idea of what to expect.

Regular Meetings: This is exactly what it sounds like – your scheduled, run-of-the-mill meeting. They are scheduled in the bylaws and follow the outline you just read.

Special Meetings: These are also known as "called meetings" and they are held when the group has urgent business that cannot wait until the next meeting. Some bylaws prohibit special meetings altogether. If your bylaws do allow for special meetings, there will be an order in terms of how the meeting will be called, such as by whom and when. A special meeting will follow the same guidelines as a regular meeting but will include only the business that was in the notice, nothing else.

Adjourned Meeting: This is a continuation of a meeting that for one reason or another was not finished. These meetings will pick up where the previous meeting left off and will follow regular meeting guidelines.

Annual Meeting: Not all organizations have annual meetings. They are not considered regular meetings. Rather, they are commonly used to elect officers or board members.

Executive Session: This is a secret or exclusive meeting. Only certain classes and members are invited and nonmembers are excluded altogether. The type of business discussed at these meetings usually deals solely with board members. A good example of an organization that utilizes this type of meeting is a fraternal society.

Quorum: There will be meetings that people miss, perhaps due to sickness or bad weather. The bylaws might state that a meeting must have half the organization's members present to continue. If the time for the meeting approaches and fewer than half the members are present, you can motion to reschedule the meeting. Your bylaws will contain the procedure you must follow to reschedule a meeting. It is similar to calling a special meeting; for instance, a good-faith effort to reach everyone should be made and everyone must be given the appropriate lead time to make the necessary changes to their schedules.

Now that you know the different types of meetings and what is to be discussed at each, you can start creating a list of everything you can think of that would be considered business in reference to your organization and its purpose. Keep in mind that every organization is different; if your club wants to start and maintain a community garden, your business can be about what seeds and plants to include and whether to expand. Robert's Rules is meant to work for any type of organization; it simply ensures that all your members are heard and given the opportunity to share ideas.

How often you meet depends on the purpose of your club. For some organizations, once a month is sufficient, while others need to meet twice a month because they keep going over their time limit. Think about what you want to accomplish and set your meeting length and times based on this. That way, you will reduce the chances of having unfinished business and running out of time. Be realistic with your time limits; remember that people have lives outside the organization. If you are overzealous about the length and frequency of meetings, members might find the club to be too demanding.

Chapter 4
Motions Explained

You have read the word "motion" many times now, but it is not what we think of in terms of the word's traditional definition. Motions in terms of meetings refer to how members express themselves. They do this by making motions in a meeting. Motions are proposals on which the entire group can take a stand.

The Four Types of Motions:

Main: This type of motion introduces items to the floor for members' consideration. Main motions cannot be made or introduced when another motion is still on the floor or is being debated.

Subsidiary: The goal of this motion is to affect or change the way a main motion is being handled. This motion will be voted on before the main motion so the proper direction can be taken into consideration and incorporated appropriately.

Privileged: These motions are used when items are more urgent, special, or important but are unrelated to other items of business. Often, these motions are about time-sensitive issues.

Incidental: The purpose of this type of motion is to allow for questions regarding other motions. Incidental motions must also be considered before the motion to which they refer.

This is how motions are presented during a meeting:

Obtaining the floor:

Wait until the previous speaker is finished. Rise and address the chairman by saying, "Mr. Chairman or Mr. President." Then wait until the chairman recognizes you.

Make your motion:

Be sure to speak in a precise and clear manner. All motions must be stated in an affirmative way. For instance, "I move that we . . ." not "I move that we do not. . ." This sounds negative and meetings are not set up to move on from that format as seamlessly as an affirmative statement. Be sure to stay on topic and avoid personalities.

Wait for someone to second your motion. Either someone will voluntarily second your motion or the chairman will call for a second.

If there is not a second to the motion, it is considered lost.

The chairman will state your motion:

The chairman will say, "It has been moved and seconded that we. . ." When that happens, your motion has been placed before the group for consideration and subsequent action. Next, the membership will either debate the motion or go directly to the vote if there is no debate. When the motion has been presented to the membership by the chairman, it is known as "assembly property," which means you cannot change it without the members' consent.

Expanding the motion:

This is when you speak to the members about your motion. You will tell them of the benefits of the motion or any other important information. You, as the mover, are always allowed to speak first, but all debates and questions must be directed at the chairman. You will have a time limit, so keep your speech to the time allotted. You will be able to speak again once everyone else who wants to speak does so unless you are called upon by the chairman to answer a question or for clarity. The question will then be put to the membership when the chairman asks, "Are you ready to vote on the motion?" As long as there is no more discussion, the vote will be taken.

Voting on a Motion:

The way in which the group votes on a motion depends on the bylaws and the situation. The five ways to vote on a motion are:

Voice: This is the most common. It is when the chairman asks, "Those in favor, say 'Aye'" or "Those opposed, say 'No.'"

Roll Call: The secretary will call each person by name. Each person will answer "yes" or "no" to the motion. This is the method used when every member is required to vote.

General Consent: This method is used when the motion is unlikely to have any opposition. The chairman will say, "If there is no objection." Silence is how the members show their agreement, but if someone says "I object," the motion will be put to a more traditional vote.

Division: This is a variation on the voice vote, as members are asked to speak, stand, or raise their hands. A count is not necessary unless the chairman asks for one.

Ballot: This is like any other ballot voting. Members will write their votes on a slip of paper. The slips of paper are then counted. This method is usually used when anonymity is needed.

Regardless of the voting process, the results of the voting will determine whether the motion is adopted. Some voting methods work better than others based on circumstances like the size of the meeting and whether the motion is likely to face opposition. If the motion is something that will benefit everyone and that fact is obvious, chances are the general consent technique will be best.

Two motions are related to voting:

Motion to table: This motion is considered an attempt to kill or stop a motion. The option to table a motion is always present, but to "take from the table," or when reconsidering, is up to the membership.

Motion to postpone indefinitely: This motion allows those opposing the motion to test their strength without having to go through the actual voting process. If this motion goes through, debate on the main motion will be reopened to the floor.

Following the correct procedure will ensure that your meetings run smoothly and efficiently. Make sure you proceed in the correct order and that members are given the floor at the correct time. When you are addressing the membership, speak clearly and precisely. You may find it scary or intimidating the first time, but wasting time will not help your cause. Before you introduce your motion, jot down some notes or make an outline of the important points. This will help you stay on track when you have a limited amount of speaking time.

Practicing the correct word choice is a good idea because it might not come as naturally to you as it does to other people. This will be especially helpful if you end up being a temporary officer, such as secretary or president. Others will also come to you with any number of questions and the more of them you can answer, the better. After all, it is not just your first time with Robert's Rules; most people have not had to use them, so other people are learning just as you are.

When presiding over a meeting, know what you're doing; if you don't, the result can be a confusing and even unfair proceeding. For the chair to be impartial and fair, he or she must know how to lead the meeting in the proper direction and balance the pros and cons. Members must make informed decisions and for them to do so, the chair must make sure all viewpoints are represented and brought up. Keep this in mind when you are making your bylaws because when it comes time for you to appoint someone else as an officer, that person will have a reliable source to fall back on.

Chapter 5
Creating Successful Committees

You know that during a meeting, time is set aside for the various committees to discuss their business matters. However, that does not mean you understand what a committee really is or what purpose it serves. Each organization is different and its needs will determine what kind of committees should be formed.

A committee is responsible for and capable of doing only what the organization asks of it. Committees are not allowed to act independently of the organization, but if a committee does have an idea it thinks will benefit the membership, it is free to bring it up to the group as a motion. The bylaws should contain the procedure necessary to create a committee, such as who has the power to appoint members. Whoever has the power to do this also has the ability to appoint the committee's chairman and to fill vacancies, if need be.

The secretary will tell members when they are appointed to a committee and will also give the committee chairman all the documents necessary to complete their tasks. When a motion is referred to a specific committee, which can happen if the motion is related to a certain committee's goals, the secretary will give the chairman a copy of the motion and the instructions that accompany it. Doing this sets the committee up for success and reduces the chances of confusion in regards to what is supposed to get done.

It is the responsibility of the committee chairman to keep all the documents given to him or her and, once the task or motion is completed, to return them in the same condition. Standing committees must keep a record of all their activities; this will be a continuous record that will be given to the new committee chairman when one is elected, which usually happens once a year.

Standing committees: These are the committees that are included in the bylaws and that are thought to be a permanent fixture within the organization. Even though the committee is permanent, the members usually change once a year when a new chairman is appointed or when new officers are elected. However, the function and purpose of the committee remain the same.

A standing committee's function is to keep harmony within the organization and its operations. When the membership or the board receives business or a motion associated with a committee, that motion or piece of business will be given to the corresponding committee to complete. It is then the committee's responsibility to complete the task or to investigate and then report back to the board, membership, or chairman.

Examples of common standing committees are:

Auditing Committee: This is a watchdog group. Even the smallest groups with limited funds should appoint a committee that is responsible for reviewing the treasurer's financial records. This committee would be in charge of checking accuracy and making sure the funds are disbursed appropriately. This type of committee is usually appointed by the chair or executive board and reports during an annual meeting. The treasurer cannot be a member of this committee because this would be a conflict of interest.

Nominating Committee: This kind of committee is usually created to suggest qualified candidates for offices within the organization. The membership generally elects members into this committee; the president or chairman cannot be an ex officio member.

Finance Committee: Whether this committee is necessary depends on the needs of the organization. A financial committee is responsible for exactly what you think – finances. This committee is responsible for creating a budget based on the financial resources and obligations of the organization. Based on these factors, this committee can make recommendations about financial matters that will benefit everyone.

Membership Committee: This type of committee is not as common as the others on the list, but some organizations are more limiting in their membership. This committee is responsible for considering and recommending members. This committee will usually keep a detailed record of membership retention and admission of new members. It will also evaluate and recruit prospective members. The members of this committee are usually appointed by the board.

Again, standing committees are based on the needs and purpose of the organization. For instance, a neighborhood organization might have standing committees that deal with things like deed restrictions, zoning, or beautification in addition to the issues mentioned above. The variations on committees are endless.

Tip: If you feel like your organization is constantly facing a need to deal with a specific issue or subject matter, it might be helpful to establish a standing committee dedicated to dealing with that issue.

Special Committee: This is also called an ad hoc or select committee. It is created when a specific task must be dealt with. Once the committee has achieved its goal, the committee is dissolved and a final report is given to the chairman and in some cases the membership as well. If a standing committee can deal with the subject or issue, a special committee should not be formed.

Special committees have two functions. The first is to investigate. For instance, if your organization wants to build its own clubhouse and is looking at potential locations, a member could make a motion to create a committee to do this. The committee would then scout locations and look into contractors, coming back to the membership with a list of options for both, including prices and a list of pros and cons. The second function of special committees is to carry out an action. Imagine that the membership agreed on one of the pieces of land and decided to purchase it. A motion could be made to create a committee to do so. Again, once the purchase went through, a final report would be given and the committee would no longer be needed because it had successfully carried out its task.

The purpose of a committee determines its size and who is chosen to serve on it. For instance, if a committee is formed to investigate a question, it is imperative that all the members' different views be represented within the committee. This allows many differences to be addressed within the committee instead of during a regular meeting, which will save a lot of time. These types of committees are usually on the large side, so all viewpoints are represented.

When a committee has been formed to carry out a specific task that the membership adopted, only those who were in favor should be on the committee. Including members who were opposed to the action could delay or even prevent the task from being carried out. This type of special committee is generally small, which works better because there are fewer schedules to coordinate. The members can meet with each other easily and get the work done quickly.

Chairman:

On both standing and special committees, the most important member is the chairman. This person is responsible for overseeing the work and calling the committee meetings. The board or the president typically appoints a committee chairman, but sometimes the membership will elect a committee chairman. It depends on the situation and bylaws.

When choosing a committee chairman, it is important to pick someone who is enthusiastic about the purpose and work of the committee. Also, pay attention to how much time a person can devote to the committee and the work. This might seem like common sense, but it is important that the person knows how to do the work. For instance, you wouldn't want someone who has never held a hammer to be responsible for building a shed. The other members of the committee should be chosen based on the skills or talents they can contribute to the group. Also, make sure to pick people who work well within a team. Even special committees are still groups; they might dissolve, but until the task is complete, it is still a form of teamwork.

In general, the bigger the organization, the more necessary it is for different committees. This is because it takes more work to make a larger organization run smoothly than it does for a small one. Committees are often thought of as the workhorses of the membership. They are the ones in charge of completing certain tasks and accomplishing various goals. To make the best of a committee, people appointed to the committee should each bring something unique to the table. Combining the talents of others in a way that will benefit the organization is a great tool for success. Without committees, an organization would not be able to accomplish much, which is why committees are so important.

Committee Business:

A common complaint about meetings is that they are long and people leave feeling like nothing was really accomplished. This is how Robert's Rules helps streamline the process, allowing even the largest of groups to get things done. A committee meeting will work the same way a regular membership meeting does. The chairman is in charge of conducting the meeting which prevents someone else from taking charge and hijacking the meeting.

The chairman of the committee calls a meeting and, just like with a regular meeting, the time, date, place, and purpose should all be included in the notice. However, if the chairman fails to do this, two members of the committee can join forces to call a meeting. If this happens, it usually means the wrong person was appointed chairman. The people who appointed the chairman should be alerted to the situation to prevent further delays.

Once the committee has been notified of the purpose and the meeting, it is up to the chairman to come prepared with an agenda. The agenda should start with the most important items of business and end with the least important. It should be set up this way in case the members run out of time or need to go home; in such a case, the most important business would have already been addressed.

Calling a committee meeting is handled in the same way as a regular meeting. In small committees, the chairman will also be the acting secretary, but for larger committees a secretary might be appointed. Either way, the minutes are kept track of. This is crucial, as it provides a record of the decisions made by the committee for others to read and to help the committee stay on track. The committee's work can help others who are faced with similar tasks in the future.

The chairman will announce the topics on the agenda so the members know what is expected of them at all times. All discussions during the meeting should be limited to the topics or the agenda. It is the responsibility of the chairman to remind members of the topic should the conversation stray. This is important because time is limited and a lot needs to be achieved in a small amount of time.

Just like in a regular meeting, the chairman of a committee must know when to cut off a discussion to move on to new topics. Robert's Rules prevents the chairman from limiting the debate because everyone is allowed to speak. However, if people are repeating themselves, the chairman can ask, "Does anyone have something new to add?" This can happen in a committee meeting as well, and the chairman should react appropriately.

Motions are not necessary in a committee meeting but can be used if necessary. The reason that might not be necessary is that some committees are small enough that everyone knows the issue, so the chairman can simply jump directly to a vote. For instance, a committee is faced with choosing a speaker for a banquet dinner and the chairman sees that most people are leaning towards the mayor. The chairman can assume a motion and say, "All those in favor of the mayor speaking, say 'Aye.'" The chairman can then say, "Those opposed, say 'No.' The 'Ayes' have it, so the motion is carried. Our committee can now invite the mayor to be the speaker."

Continuing with this example, if the chairman feels that the members are not leaning towards a speaker, he or she can ask, "Would a member like to make a motion about who we should invite to be our speaker at the banquet?" This will leave it up to the members of the committee to provide a motion.

It is important to have either a traditional motion or to assume a motion because that way everyone knows exactly what they are agreeing to. This will reduce the chances of confusion. Back to the previous example, people might claim that they agreed to the governor speaking, not the mayor. However, if a motion was used, it would have been recorded and a simple reading of the records would reflect that fact.

Before the meeting ends, the chairman should provide a summary of what was accomplished in the meeting and summarize any assignments given to members as well as how long members have to complete them. This should also be recorded by the chairman or the secretary in the minutes so that the chairman can keep track of how the work is progressing. A permanent record can also be used to help future members or chairmen.

It is important to note that both standing and special committees are equally important and should be treated as such. Even if the committee will dissolve once the task is complete, members should not slack off on the work because they think it is not as important as committees that are permanent parts of an organization.

When you are writing the bylaws for your organization, think about the direction you want to go with your organization. For instance, think about how large your membership will be based on factors such as where you live and how popular you think the organization will be. This will help you create committees of an appropriate size.

It is also a good idea to get your calculator and do the math. Based on the dues you set and your projected number of members, you can set a ballpark figure of the budget you are dealing with. Also, consider the goals and obligations you have in mind for your organization, as your committee will reflect this in both size and members.

In addition, think about how you are going to publicize your group and whether you will need a standing committee that deals with memberships. Are you going to have a list of requirements for potential members, or are you going to accept anyone who wants to join as long as they pay the dues? Having a standing committee, even a small one, involved with all aspects of the membership process is a good idea because it will keep the organization more organized and efficient.

Take your time and feel free to be creative when it comes to brainstorming ideas for standing committees. After all, they are the real workers of the organization, which means more work will get done. If you are starting an organization, make sure to listen to everyone's opinions and ideas. Even something that might seem odd or unimportant at first can turn out to be a constant issue. It is easier to come up with the committees and include them in the bylaws so that their rules are already set than it is to add a standing committee later.

Chapter 6
Roles and Responsibilities

By now you have probably figured out that there are different officers and officials within an organization, each with his or her own set of responsibilities. Even if you do not plan on holding any of these positions, it is in your best interest to understand what each of them do. Chances are, if you are starting your own organization, you will be chairman or president, at least at the beginning, and until things start running smoothly, you might find yourself wearing many hats. Being the one to start the organization means people will come to you with different questions, especially regarding their specific roles. The more you know how to do things, the better.

Typically, officers are selected from the organization's membership, but in some cases, the president or other officers are nonmembers. When an organization is dealing with a controversial issue, it might seek the services of a nonmember. These nonmembers are often called "professional presiding officers," and their positions are usually temporary. They generally leave once the issue is resolved and the organization returns to its more traditional method of using only members as officers.

Officers and committee chairs are responsible for keeping detailed records of all assignments and tasks; these records will then be given to their successors. Some organizations have a headquarters or facility; if this is the case, all minutes, checkbooks, society records, and investment records should be kept there. Some smaller organizations allow officers to take their records home with them, but as many people find out, this is a bad idea because sometimes people will simply stop coming to the meetings – a big deal if that person is your treasurer and has the organization's checkbook.

If your organization does have a facility, make sure to give both the treasurer and the secretary an area for each of them to conduct their work. Some small organizations have a designated box or crate in which all officers are required to deposit their records (or, in the case of the treasurer, the checkbook). This way everything stays together and can be easily carried to and from the meetings.

When you elect officers, think about how well that person will fit the role. Think about how reliable the person is and whether you think he or she will take the position seriously. The people who are nominated must be honest with themselves about how much time they can safely devote to the job and whether it fits into their schedules before they accept the position upon winning the election. During a term, if an officer finds that he or she simply cannot handle all the responsibilities of the position, the officer can ask others for help or resign from the position. If the officer resigns, all records and documents should be returned with the officer's letter of resignation.

Even the smallest organizations require a minimum of two officers: a secretary and a president. This is because the president will preside at the meetings and the secretary will record the minutes. These two things are the absolute minimum, but for some smaller organizations, they are enough to ensure that things run smoothly. Regardless of the organization, the bylaws dictate what authority the president has and that it is not a free-reign dictatorship situation like most people assume.

Common Officers

Chairman or President: This is the presiding officer, usually referred to as the president or the chairman. However, sometimes a special title is given to this person; for instance, in religious assemblies this individual is known as the moderator. During a meeting, the appropriate title will always be used, with the appropriate prefix of Mr. or Madam. When referring to themselves, they will usually say "the chair" and not their name regardless of whether the position is permanent or temporary.

In most professional and social organizations, the president is considered the most important officer when it comes to the action and purpose of the organization. When this is the case, presidential candidates might have their own platforms. Members then allow the goals, philosophies, and plans of the candidates to influence their votes.

Other organizations have bylaws that limit the power of the president to simply presiding over the meetings, leaving any actual legislative power to an executive board. Again, when it comes to your organization, you probably have an idea of how you want it to operate. Choose the option that works best for your vision.

One of the most important administrative duties of the president is to represent the organization. This means that the president is the one who will sign the legal documents, speak for the organization when necessary, and preside over the meetings. Sometimes organizations will also have employees for special events, and it is the president who organizes them and oversees their work. Duties will vary based on the bylaws, but these are the most common.

President

You already know how the president interacts with the members during a meeting, but there are three main duties of the president:

Keep order.

Be impartial and fair.

Protect the rights of the members.

Keeping order is what Robert's Rules is meant to do. Only one person should speak at a time and no one should be angry because they have been overlooked. If the president is making sure the members are following the rules and is keeping them on track, this is relatively easy. The president should be keeping an eye out for any member who is standing up. This seems like a strange thing to do, but it is part of the president's duty to ask someone why he or she is rising. Doing so in a timely manner will help move the meeting forward and keep everyone on topic.

When it comes to being fair and impartial, the president must remember that he or she represents the entire membership. The president is not allowed to represent only those he or she agrees with. This is important because during the meeting it is up to the president to make sure that all viewpoints, pros, and cons are addressed. If the president fails to do this, the membership will not make an informed decision based on all the facts.

To ensure fairness, the president must adhere to the following rules:

- During a meeting, the president is not allowed to enter the debate or make motions.

If the president wants to enter the debate, he or she must first hand the chair over to the vice president or a different officer. Doing this means that the president will no longer preside over the meeting and cannot return to the chair until the motion has been resolved. The president is also required to hand the chair over to someone else when there is a conflict of interest, such as direct monetary gain.

- The president can vote if it would break a tie, create a tie vote, or if the vote is taken by ballot.

- The president must help members properly phrase motions, even if the president is opposed to the motion itself. It is inappropriate for a president to say that a member is wrong or lying. Instead, when the president is correcting false information, he or she must phrase it as, "The chair has information that. . ."

- If possible, the president should sit when someone else has the floor. If sitting is not an option, the president should stand back from the podium or lectern.

- The president is in charge of alternating between the pros and cons during a debate. This is especially important when dealing with a controversial topic.

A good president protects the rights of the members by following the rules and bylaws. The president is responsible for ensuring that members are not purposely making crazy motions or amendments. If the president sees any members engaging in undemocratic behavior that interrupts the meeting, the president will be firm but calm in doing one of two things: rule the motions out of order or choosing not to recognize the member. These are to be done only when necessary, and a president should not abuse his or her power simply to speed up a meeting. Personal feelings should not get in the way of a president doing his or her job; the president must take the wishes of the entire membership, not just a select few, into consideration. When a person is being a nuisance, the president should know the proper procedure for calling to order a specific member. Should the president need to invoke this power, he or she would say, "The member is out of order and will be seated."

Additionally, if that unruly member does not sit down after the president's instructions to do so, the person's behavior can be recorded in the minutes. The president can also call out the offender by name; this is known as "preferring charges." It is considered a last resort and should be treated as such by the president. However, if the president does have to prefer charges, he or she must state what the member has done and the membership will decide what happens next. If no one voluntarily comes forth with a motion, the president can ask, "What penalty should be imposed on the member?" It is now up to the membership to propose a penalty.

As with other motions, this, too, is debatable, and even the member facing the penalty is given the opportunity to speak. This type of motion will be taken by a majority vote unless the penalty involves taking away rights, in which case it would require a two-thirds vote instead.

The president should exhaust all other options before resorting to preferring charges. Another option is for the president to declare a recess and to speak with the member privately to see if they can't solve the problem together.

Not everyone is comfortable being president; some people make better leaders than others based on personality traits and qualities. Some of the most important qualities are:

Judgment: This can be important because it can help with the flow of business; for instance, someone with good judgment knows when being strict helps and when it hinders.

Learning: This one is often overlooked, but eagerness to learn is not something that can be faked. As a matter of fact, it is generally very easy to tell if someone possesses this quality, and it will make it easier to teach them the correct procedures.

Listening: This is important for obvious reasons. The president will be listening to the membership during meetings. However, listening can also include body language and the ability to pick up on signals that members are giving, then responding to them in a constructive and appropriate way.

Calmness: Being president is not without its stressors and it can be stressful at times. The president should not have a quick temper, but rather keep his or her cool in the face of turbulence.

Humility: Sometimes members will point out what the president is doing wrong. If the president is not good at handling criticism, this can cause tension. However, if the president takes these criticisms and learns from them, the environment will be more peaceful and harmonious.

Firmness: This trait is important because members might not always stay on track; it will be up to the president to keep everyone on course.

Vice President

This office is often thought of as a president-in-training because filling in for the president when necessary is one of the most important duties of the vice president. This can happen for any number of reasons, but it is assumed that the vice president will take over the office if the president must step down for any reason. Some organizations might have more than one vice president; if this is the case, the order of succession should be specified in the bylaws.

When the vice president is filling in for the president, the vice president should be addressed as though he or she were the president. However, when both the vice president and president are present, the vice president should be called "Madam Vice President" or "Mr. Vice President." Some organizations prefer not to use "Mr. Chairman" or "Madam Chairman" instead, so if in doubt, this is usually acceptable.

The bylaws will contain a detailed list of the vice president's responsibilities. For instance, a common duty is to preside over motions involving the formation of special committees. However, this is just an example, as the needs of the organization will determine the specific duties of the vice president. The vice president is still an important office and should be taken seriously. Some people assume the position will not be time consuming or difficult, but this is simply not true. The vice president is responsible for learning about and following the correct procedures. He or she is basically the on-call president and is expected to act like it, which means representing the organization in a positive manner.

Secretary

Remember that this officer is half of the bare minimum required to properly run an organization and a meeting. This goes to show how important the role of secretary really is. Some people argue that the secretary is even more important than the president because of the amount of work that goes into the position. The secretary is responsible for preparing the agenda, keeping track of the organization's records, managing correspondence, mailing notices of meetings, recording and taking minutes, and any other administrative duties the bylaws state.

Minutes:

Many people are not sure what goes into the minutes, and to be honest, each organization might have different needs based on its bylaws. However, in general, the minutes are a record of what was done during the meeting, not what was said, like many people assume. The assembly will typically approve and correct the minutes; if the secretary makes a mistake, he or she can correct it by bringing it to the attention of the assembly. When this occurs, a motion will be made to amend the minutes; generally, there is no opposition and this can take a quick general consent vote.

If the bylaws specify that the minutes be typed, in addition to the usual information, when a question is asked, a list of the speakers should be included.

Structure of Minutes

Call to Order:

Organization name.

List of present officers.

Roll call if specified in the bylaws. If this is necessary, it is important to note who is present and who is absent, as well as whether someone leaves early or arrives late.

Approval of the minutes from the previous meeting:

Any actions taken on the minutes, such as corrections. The approval of the minutes will be specified here, both with or without corrections. If corrections were made, approval will come after the mistake was corrected.

Body:

Reports of committees and officers: This section will contain reports of boards, officers, and both standing and special committees, including their agendas and actions taken to achieve the desired tasks. What is included in the treasurer's report is determined by the bylaws or the membership; it will typically include the beginning balance, ending balance, total income, and total expenditures.

Special orders: This is where nominations and elections should be recorded. The secretary should pay special attention to names and dates, as this is crucial for filling officer positions at the correct times. Remember, some bylaws limit how long someone can hold a certain office, and if the secretary does not keep track of who was elected when, confusion may result and the bylaws may not be followed properly.

Unfinished business: The name of the person who made the motion and the final wording of ALL the main motions, as well as any motions that pose a question to the assembly. The results of each motion should also be recorded here. In addition, any motion that was adopted should be recorded. Secondary motions like the motion to recess should be included in this section, along with the name of the members who were recessed and the exact time at which the meeting was called back to order.

Speaker: If there is a special speaker, this is where their name and program name should be recorded.

Previous notice: All previous notices should be recorded here. This includes when someone gives previous notice to amend an earlier action.

Announcements: This is where announcements will be recorded, including any dates and locations that are important regarding the announcement.

These should be included as they come up during the meeting:

Any tallies of votes or ballots.

Record of any appeals or points of order, as well as the chair's ruling.

Adjournment:

This will be the last paragraph of the minutes. It should contain the time of adjournment followed by the signature of the secretary. Some bylaws state that the president must also sign after the secretary, but this is not a requirement unless otherwise specified.

Treasurer

The treasurer is responsible for keeping track of dues and expenditures. For small organizations, this can be relatively easy and the treasurer can give his or her report orally. The job gets progressively more complex and difficult as the organization gets bigger because larger clubs generally have other sources of income and more expenditures than do smaller organizations.

General duties:

Giving and keeping receipts.

Depositing money into the club's bank account. The treasurer should not have the organization's money in his or her own account.

Delivering the report in the desired manner at meetings.

Paying the bills that the membership has voted to pay. This should be done according to the bylaws. Generally, the treasurer will use the organization's checkbook, but some clubs still prefer to deal with cash only.

Managing the records so that the committee can audit the books at the designated time. Examples of this are which members have paid their dues and when they did so, and when bills are due.

Keeping track of the checking account and making sure it is kept reconciled and balanced.

In larger organizations, the treasurer is also responsible for payroll if there are paid employees. This includes deducting both income and social security taxes. If the club owns property, it is up to the treasurer to file state, federal, and local taxes. The treasurer might also be responsible for submitting a budget report for approval; the procedure for this would be detailed in the bylaws.

When it comes to large organizations, the treasurer is generally required to deliver the report, but also turn in a hard copy. Some larger organizations also want the treasurer to be bonded so that the organization is protected from loss. This should also be in the bylaws.

After learning about what each of the officers is required to do, you might be thinking twice about accepting any of these positions. Even if someone is nominated, he or she doesn't have to accept the position. If a person doesn't think he or she can handle the responsibility or devote enough time to the office, it is better that the person passes it up so that someone who does have the time can take the position. This will be better for the club and will make things run more smoothly.

By now you have probably figured out that the bylaws are the most important document in your organization. The bylaws are the foundation upon which your club sits and they can set you up for either success or failure. This will depend on what you include in them. After reading about what the different offices are required to do, you should have a better understanding of what the bylaws should contain with respect to each office.

Robert's Rules of Order should make much more sense to you now that you have a working understanding of them. They are meant to bring organization and fairness to any club's meetings. Some people say that learning the Rules is one of the most difficult aspects of starting a club and running a meeting. It is for this reason that so many people hold classes to teach new members the basics. This way, members won't feel so overwhelmed and confused when they join and begin attending meetings.

The good news is that you are now equipped with all the tools you need for a successful journey. You should feel more confident now when it comes to constructing your bylaws and knowing which personality traits to look for in a potential president. Now it is up to you to take everything you have learned and create the organization you envisioned.

www.ingramcontent.com/pod-product-compliance
Lightning Source LLC
Chambersburg PA
CBHW070105210526
45170CB00013B/756